BIRDS vs. BLADES?

OFFSHORE WIND POWER AND THE RACE TO PROTECT SEABIRDS

REBECCA E. HIRSCH

M MILLBROOK PRESS · MINNEAPOLIS

To all those who've ever watched a bird and wondered where it was going

Millbrook Press™
An imprint of Lerner Publishing Group, Inc.
241 First Avenue North
Minneapolis, MN 55401 USA

For reading levels and more information, look up this title at www.lernerbooks.com.

Main body text set in Avenir Book.
Typeface provided by Linotype AG.

Library of Congress Cataloging-in-Publication Data

Names: Hirsch, Rebecca E., author.
Title: Birds vs. blades? : offshore wind power and the race to protect seabirds / by Rebecca E. Hirsch.
Other titles: Birds versus blades?
Description: Minneapolis : Millbrook Press, [2017] | Includes bibliographical references and index.
Identifiers: LCCN 2015044328 (print) | LCCN 2015045865 (ebook) | ISBN 9781467795203 (lb : alk. paper) | ISBN 9781512411119 (eb pdf)
Subjects: LCSH: Sea birds—Juvenile literature. | Coastal ecology—Juvenile literature. | Offshore wind power plants—Environmental aspects—Juvenile literature. | Wind power—Environmental aspects—Juvenile literature.
Classification: LCC QL678.52 .H57 2017 (print) | LCC QL678.52 (ebook) | DDC 578.77—dc23

LC record available at http://lccn.loc.gov/2015044328

Manufactured in the United States of America
2-52429-20633-2/28/2022

CONTENTS

CHAPTER 1
AN OCEAN MYSTERY

Above the Atlantic Ocean, a few miles from the New Jersey shore, a large white bird glides on black-tipped wings. It scans the waves below and spies a school of herring. In an instant, the bird points itself downward and plummets toward the water. Just before impact, it folds its wings straight back. It spears the water like an arrow.

Underwater, the bird flaps its wings and kicks its webbed feet through the swarm of fish. It snatches a silver fish in its beak, swallows, and bobs to the surface. Water rolls off its wings as the bird returns to the sky.

The northern gannet is one of the animal world's extreme athletes, a bird known for graceful flight and high-speed dives. Like all seabirds, northern gannets are built for ocean travel. Catching the wind on wings that reach nearly 6.6 feet (2 meters) across, gannets sail over the waves and travel long distances with ease. The structure of their wings, bent at the elbow and tapered to a point, is perfect for gliding on ocean gusts. "High wind

Diving gannets hit the water at speeds of more than 60 miles (97 kilometers) per hour. They can stay underwater for up to thirty seconds in pursuit of fish.

doesn't bother them," explains scientist Iain Stenhouse. "They're made for it."

But seabirds' deep connection to ocean wind could become a problem. Soon they may need to share their airspace with something else that is made for wind: wind farms.

A wind farm is a cluster of towering wind turbines (windmills) each as tall as a thirty-story building. Propeller-like blades catch the wind and spin a generator, which makes

Seabirds are a diverse group, including any bird that depends largely on the marine environment. Seabirds range from emperor penguins *(above)* to tiny arctic terns *(below)*, which migrate from near the North Pole to Antarctica.

electricity. Wind power is a form of clean energy, because it makes electricity without creating air pollution.

Experts think the US Atlantic coast is a great place to harvest wind energy. In 2015 workers began building five wind turbines for the first wind farm in US waters, 3 miles (5 km) off the coast of Rhode Island. More offshore wind projects are planned for Massachusetts, New Jersey, Maryland, and Virginia. But these same waters are the winter home for millions of seabirds, including the northern gannet. Scientists worry that sharing space with wind farms could be disastrous for seabirds.

Studying a bird that lives over the ocean is difficult, so the lives of seabirds largely remain a mystery. To protect these birds from wind farms, scientists must learn more about how they use the Atlantic Ocean. *What migration paths do they follow? Where do they fish and travel? How much do their travel patterns shift from year to year?*

Are offshore wind farms safe for seabirds? No one is sure. As this clean-energy technology comes face-to-face with offshore wildlife, scientists are racing to learn all they can about seabirds and find ways to keep them safe.

LIFE AT SEA

All seabirds spend their days hunting. Northern gannets *(left)* look for fish in the water as they soar over the waves. They may also follow fishing boats for discards, watch for other birds feeding, or look for whales driving fish to the surface. According to biologist Iain Stenhouse, "When they find food, they wheel around above, sometimes in dense chaotic flocks, and plunge into the water . . . to attack the prey."

Some seabirds dive from the water's surface. Scoters, a kind of sea duck, eat mussels and oysters. Scoters gather in flocks on the water over shellfish beds. They dive to the bottom, rest on the water while they digest their meal, and then dive again.

At night seabirds rest. They come to sheltered spots with calmer waters and sleep on the water. Although not much is known about how they sleep, Stenhouse says they probably stay alert, perhaps occasionally opening one or both eyes to watch for danger.

Offshore wind farms generate renewable power from strong ocean winds several miles from shore. Scientists are studying seabirds' flight patterns to make sure offshore wind won't threaten the birds.

CHAPTER 2
INTO THE FOG

On a rainy March evening, three scientists in a white pickup truck drive through Cape Charles, Virginia, to the harbor at the edge of town. The harbor sits at the mouth of the Chesapeake Bay, which stretches 200 miles (322 km) inland from the Atlantic Ocean. In the summer, the harbor is a bustling place. People come to fish, sail, and water-ski. Yet in winter, few people visit. The harbor is deserted as the white pickup rolls into the parking lot.

The truck doors open and wildlife biologists Carrie Gray, Carl Anderson, and Robby Lambert climb out. They stop for a moment and look out at the bay.

"Looks foggy out there," Gray remarks.

Anderson, who will pilot the boat, walks to the edge of the wooden pier, surveys the bay, and returns. "We've probably got about a half mile [0.8 km] of visibility. I'll just have to see what it looks like when we get out there."

Catching birds in a fog is nearly impossible, but the fog is supposed to lift later tonight. The scientists will try their luck and head into the fog.

This nighttime mission is part of a large investigation. In 2012 a group of scientists, working with the Bureau of Ocean Energy Management and the US Fish and Wildlife Service, launched a seabird research project. Their goal was to track the movements of bird species that could be at risk from wind farms. They planned to capture birds on the water, implant them with high-tech tags, and release them, so that the scientists could follow the tagged birds and learn the secrets of their movements.

If scientists could tag enough seabirds and watch their movements over time, they could learn the migration pathways and day-to-day movements for each species. The more of each

The boat must be just the right size for catching seabirds: big enough to stand up to waves but small enough for a netter to scoop a sleeping bird off the water.

species they could catch and tag, the more data they could study and the more confident they would be in the patterns they saw.

But catching birds at sea would not be easy. Researchers would have to chase down seabirds on the winter ocean at night, when the birds are sleeping on the water's surface. The work would be dark, cold, and tiring. But it would also be exciting. And what they would learn could shine a light on the lives of seabirds and help determine how these vulnerable ocean creatures can coexist safely with wind farms.

Gray, Anderson, and Lambert are hoping for an exciting night out on the bay. They zip themselves into flotation suits and jackets. They pull on warm, waterproof gloves and hats. Tonight it is rainy and mild, around 50°F (10°C), but on the water, temperatures can drop and weather conditions can change quickly. The crew must be prepared to face icy winds, freezing rain, sleet, or snow.

A 25-foot (7.6 m) powerboat is bobbing in the water. It has a canopy and steering wheel in the center and two engines in back. The scientists load their gear—a spotlight, a big net on a pole, towels, and several large plastic tubs with airholes drilled in the sides for holding captured birds. Lambert perches on the prow (the pointed front part of the boat). He sits straddling the railing, his rubber boots dangling over the water. He holds the spotlight. Gray stands behind him gripping the net. Anderson steps behind the wheel. He flips a switch, and the engines roar to life. He pilots the boat through the harbor into the bay.

The Chesapeake Bay opens into the mid-Atlantic Ocean, an ecosystem that is centered about halfway up the coast between Florida and Maine. A huge variety of marine animals depend on this rich ecosystem for their habitat, including thirty-one different species of seabirds.

The mid-Atlantic Ocean is also the site of three Wind Energy Areas (WEAs), zones identified by the US government as targets for future wind development. One WEA begins about 30 miles (48 km) from the mouth of the Chesapeake. Two others are farther north, off the coasts of Maryland and Delaware.

The WEAs are part of a clean energy revolution in the United States. Wind energy is a source of nonpolluting, renewable energy. No matter how much we use, we will never run out. The United States already has more than fifty thousand wind turbines on land. They spin over deserts, plains, and windy mountaintops.

Enormous amounts of wind energy are also found over our oceans. A few miles from shore, East Coast winds blow at an average speed of 18 to 20 miles per hour (8 to 9 m per second). But move inland, where trees,

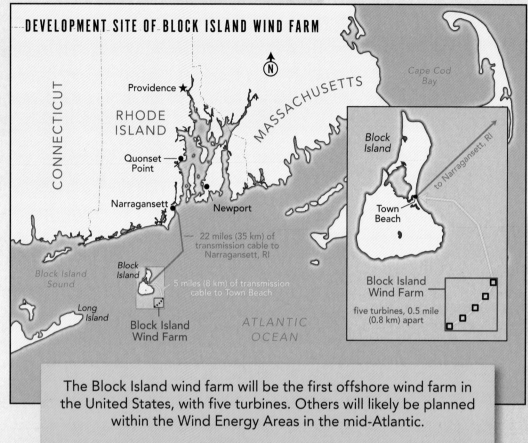

DEVELOPMENT SITE OF BLOCK ISLAND WIND FARM

The Block Island wind farm will be the first offshore wind farm in the United States, with five turbines. Others will likely be planned within the Wind Energy Areas in the mid-Atlantic.

buildings, and rocks slow the wind, and the wind speed drops to just 11 to 12 miles per hour (about 5 m per second). Ocean winds blow day and night, stronger and steadier than land winds. Wind turbines along the breezy US Atlantic coast could deliver clean electricity to huge cities like New York; Philadelphia; Baltimore; and Washington, DC.

HOW AN OFFSHORE WIND FARM WORKS

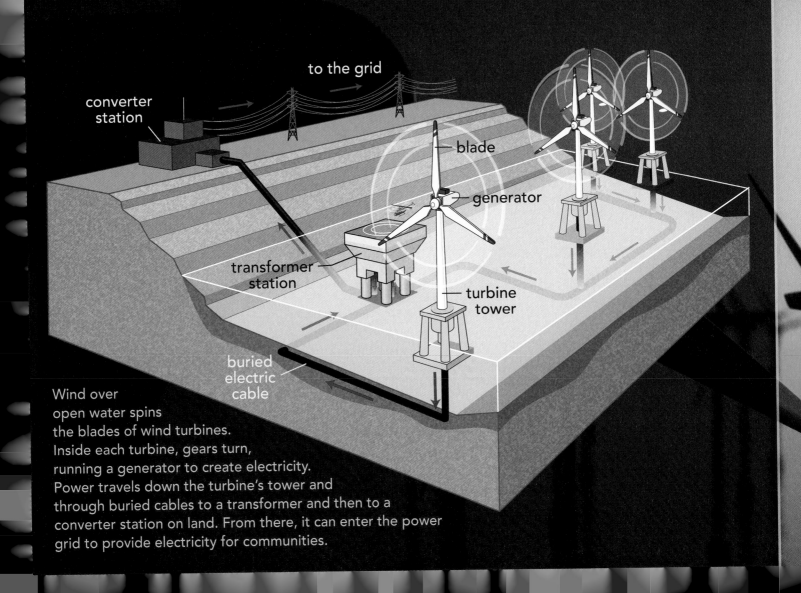

to the grid

converter
station

blade

generator

transformer
station

turbine
tower

buried
electric
cable

Wind over
open water spins
the blades of wind turbines.
Inside each turbine, gears turn,
running a generator to create electricity.
Power travels down the turbine's tower and
through buried cables to a transformer and then to a
converter station on land. From there, it can enter the power
grid to provide electricity for communities.

But wind turbines are a danger to birds. Birds can be killed in collisions with the moving blades. The tips of the spinning blades can reach speeds up to 170 miles (274 km) per hour. Some birds avoid wind farms altogether, which can prevent them from reaching nearby habitat they need. How can people harvest the power of ocean winds without harming ocean birds? Scientists think most of the risk can be avoided if we put wind farms far away from migration corridors and important bird habitats.

Yet scientists know very little about where Atlantic seabirds fly and hunt.

"We don't know the migration patterns," Anderson explains. "Where do these birds go? When do they go there? Would they be negatively affected if [people] put a large wind farm in one place or another?"

Anderson, Gray, and Lambert are capturing seabirds to answer these questions. Tonight the crew is looking for two species that could be at risk: northern gannets and red-throated loons. Like all seabirds, these birds are migrants. Northern gannets live in the Atlantic Ocean. In North America, they fly between their breeding grounds in Canada and their wintering grounds along the US Atlantic and Gulf coasts. They hunt over the continental shelf, the flat, shallow edge of the continent that is submerged under the sea.

More than fifty thousand wind turbines spin on land in the United States.

Red-throated loons live around the Northern Hemisphere. They are the smallest of all loons and the most widespread. They are nervous birds, easily frightened by anything new or unfamiliar. They breed on ponds and lakes on the Arctic tundra and spend winter on coasts farther to the south, like here in the Chesapeake.

Red-throated loons spend their lives in the water, coming to shore only to nest.

The loon's name comes from its summer coloring. It sports a deep red patch on its neck in the summer, which stands out against its gray head. In winter, its head and neck turn white and gray, and the red patch goes away.

Elsewhere in the middle Atlantic region, capture teams are out on the water looking for a third at-risk species: a black-and-white sea duck known as a surf scoter.

The male surf scoter has a boldly patterned head, giving rise to its common name, the skunk-headed coot. Surf scoters swim on the water near the shore, dive for mollusks, and feed and travel in flocks. In flight their wings whistle, so when a flock lifts off, the wingbeats fill the air with a humming sound.

In addition to the capture teams, many other scientists are involved. Kate Williams and Iain Stenhouse of the Biodiversity Research Institute are leaders on the project. A team of wildlife veterinarians wait onshore, ready to surgically implant tags on captured birds. The tags are implanted under the birds' skin because a tag on the outside of the body would interfere with the feathers, which are crucial to a seabird's survival.

SEABIRD WHO'S WHO

The research team is studying three species of Atlantic seabirds that could be vulnerable to offshore wind farms.

NORTHERN GANNET *(MORUS BASSANUS)*

More than two hundred thousand northern gannets live in North America, and more live on the eastern side of the Atlantic. Although their population is stable, many gannets die when they get tangled in fishing nets. Studies in Europe show that gannets avoid wind farms, which means more are crowded into other areas. What's more, they fly at the same height as a wind turbine's moving blades—and they fly looking down, to watch for prey in the water. So they may be at risk of collisions.

RED-THROATED LOON *(GAVIA STELLATA)*

Red-throated loons are the most widespread loon in the world. About one hundred thousand red-throated loons spend winter along the US Atlantic coast, with the largest concentration in the middle Atlantic region. In many places, the population of red-throated loons is falling, and scientists aren't sure why. Many red-throated loons drown in fishing nets. In Europe red-throated loons strongly avoid wind farms, making habitat loss a concern.

SURF SCOTER *(MELANITTA PERSPICILLATA)*

More than one million of these black-and-white sea ducks live in North America, although their population is dwindling. They breed in summer on small lakes and ponds across Canada and Alaska, and they spend winter along North American coasts. In Europe, where offshore wind farms have been in place for five to ten years, related species of sea ducks have avoided those areas. So scientists think wind farms in US waters could shrink habitat available to surf scoters.

Meanwhile, on the Chesapeake, catching birds on this night is not proving easy. All is dark as Anderson pilots the boat through the water. From his perch on the prow, Lambert turns on the spotlight. A wall of fog appears.

He sweeps the light back and forth. Flecks of rain, a short span of black water, and fog appear in the beam. In better weather, the crew would hope to shine the spotlight on a gannet or red-throated loon at rest on the water. The light disorients the bird, giving the netter a chance to scoop it up.

The crew knows that gannets and red-throated loons come with their own challenges. Red-throated loons are gentle and easy to handle but devilishly tricky to catch. When approached, the loon tends to dive, swim under the dark water, and pop up a long distance away.

Gannets, on the other hand, are easy to catch. They just sit there, "like a shoebox on the water," Anderson laughs.

"Sometimes they'll even swim toward the boat as if to say, 'You don't know what you're doing, I'm going to make this easy for you.'"

But once on board, gannets are a handful, wielding their sharp beak like a sword. "They will poke you," Anderson warns. "And they'll poke you seriously and dangerously. They will go for your eye. I have a lot of respect for these birds."

Gannets use their sharp beaks to defend themselves, which makes them challenging to handle.

The boat *thrums* through the fog. Rain spatters down. All eyes follow the beam of the spotlight across the black water, searching for seabirds. Suddenly, a peeping sound emerges from the fog. In the next moment, a gray-and-white bird appears in the light. It looks like a duck, but it is a horned grebe, another kind of seabird. Unfortunately, it is not a bird the crew is looking for. The grebe turns and paddles furiously away from the boat. The team continues into the fog, searching.

After a while, Anderson stops the boat. Everyone discusses what to do.

"It's all chance. We're not going to see them from a distance," says Anderson.

"It would be luck," says Gray. "Just blind luck."

"We're not going to catch any in the living room," Lambert offers.

Anderson steers the boat toward a stretch of shore where they caught red-throated loons the night before. Perhaps the birds will still be there. Anderson slows the boat to a crawl. Water gently slaps the sides of the boat. If they go slowly, maybe they can sneak up on the birds.

But still they have no luck. The stubborn fog remains. Finally, Gray throws up her hands. "This feels really silly."

"Not seeing much," Anderson agrees.

They are wasting expensive fuel with almost no hope of finding birds. At last, everyone agrees to turn in for the night. Anderson steers the boat back to the Cape Charles harbor.

Tomorrow they will try again.

WIND, WAVES, AND WEATHER

The next morning, a team of researchers awakens in a rental house on the outskirts of Cape Charles. The boat crew from last night is here, along with three veterinarians, the surgery team. The large house has two kitchens, a comfortable living room, and enough bedrooms for all.

Everyone is working together to catch seabirds and implant them with tracking devices. For four winters in a row, rotating crews have headed onto the water at night, with different teams working each week. They have looked for gannets and loons at three locations: here at the Chesapeake; in Delaware Bay, between Delaware and New Jersey; and in Pamlico Sound, in North Carolina. Every tagged bird helps fill in the mystery of the movements of an entire population of seabirds. This information will be essential for keeping birds safe as offshore wind farms are developed.

Crews have been at work all winter during this final year of capture missions. The Chesapeake, in March, is the crews' last stop. They have caught red-throated loons

Carl Anderson holds a red-throated loon caught in Hatteras, North Carolina.

here this year, but no gannets. Gannets roam widely during the winter, following food, and they haven't shown up in the Chesapeake yet. The crew doesn't have much time left. Soon all the winter birds will leave the middle Atlantic and wing their way north to their breeding grounds.

Anderson spends the day preparing for the upcoming night's mission. In the cold morning, he drives the white pickup to the

Part bridge and part tunnel, the Chesapeake Bay Bridge-Tunnel crosses the wide mouth of the bay. Fish arrive here in late winter and so do northern gannets.

Chesapeake Bay Bridge-Tunnel. The 20-mile (32 km) bridge includes two sections of tunnel that run underwater across busy shipping channels. Cape Charles sits on the east side of the bay. Across the bridge and through the tunnels sits Virginia Beach, on the west side of the bay.

Anderson drives partway across the bridge and pulls off toward a parking area on a rocky man-made island, near one of the tunnels. Last night's fog has lifted. Enormous ships are anchored farther up the Chesapeake. An icy wind howls across the water as Anderson sets up a spotting scope. Gulls squawk and hover over the water, but he is not interested in them. He is here to look for northern gannets. They are easy to spot. Gannets are brighter white than gulls. In flight they make a four-pointed shape: two pointy wings, a pointed head, and a pointed tail.

Soon the waters around the bridge-tunnel will become crowded with gannets. The waters of the Chesapeake warm rapidly as spring pushes its way into the bay. Fish follow the warming water, and gannets follow the fish. Anderson is here to see if the birds have arrived yet.

UP THE OCEAN FOOD WEB ◄━━━━━

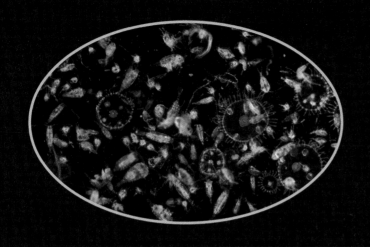

Seabirds belong to the ocean food web, a network of energy that links all ocean life. The web starts with phytoplankton. These tiny plants make their own food from sunlight. Phytoplankton are eaten by tiny animals called zooplankton *(left)*. Zooplankton are eaten by small fish, and small fish are eaten by larger fish and seabirds.

Seabirds sit at the top of the food web. Being at the top makes them sensitive to changes all along the food web. They can alert us to a change in the ocean ecosystem. If a seabird population drops in one place, it could mean the health of the entire food web is in danger.

The Chesapeake Bay is part of the Atlantic Flyway, a bird migratory highway that runs along the Atlantic coast of North America. As the longest inlet along the Atlantic Flyway, the Chesapeake is filled with food. To the north and south of the Chesapeake, smaller bays are also rich with aquatic life and birds.

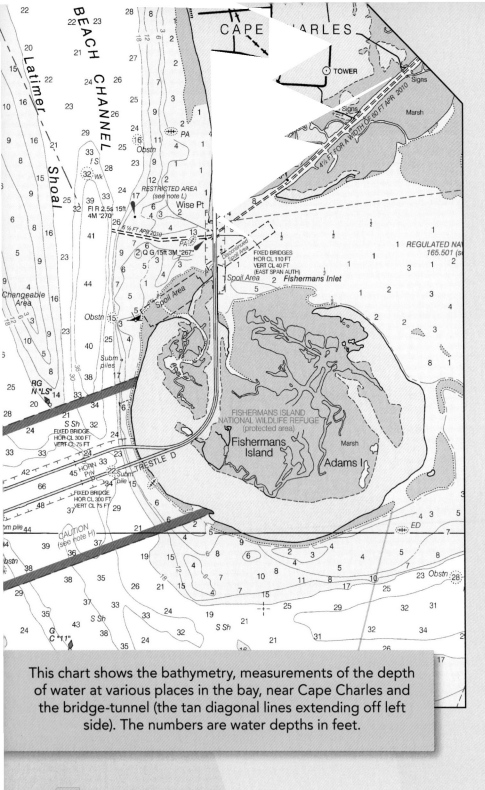

This chart shows the bathymetry, measurements of the depth of water at various places in the bay, near Cape Charles and the bridge-tunnel (the tan diagonal lines extending off left side). The numbers are water depths in feet.

Through the scope, he spies a few hungry gannets soaring over the waves. They cruise in high circles and then swoop low over the water, scanning for fish. But they aren't diving. That's a sure sign the fish haven't arrived, which explains why so few gannets are here. The timing of their arrival is part of the mystery the scientists are trying to solve.

His scouting mission complete, Anderson packs up his scope and drives back to the rental house. That afternoon he sits on the couch peering at his laptop computer. As captain, he is planning a course for tonight's capture mission. On the National Oceanic and Atmospheric Administration (NOAA) Office of Coast Survey website, he studies charts showing water depth, an important clue in the search for seabirds. He also checks weather conditions, including wind and fog.

Wind is important because the crew can't work in choppy seas. Waves higher than 3 feet (0.9 m) are too difficult and too dangerous. Whatever wave height is predicted, the waves will be a foot (0.3 m) higher near the bridge-tunnel.

Anderson knows that a range of factors can affect where to find seabirds, including water temperature, water depth, and distance from land. Gannets tend to gather near the wide mouth of the Chesapeake at the bridge-tunnel. Red-throated loons are often found along the bay's shores, where the water depth is about 20 to 30 feet (6 to 9 m). But if the crew has been working one shore for several nights, the loons there can become skittish and hard to catch. When that happens, the crew may cross over the deep central channel and search for loons on the far shore. But the central channel is also a shipping channel, so the crew won't cross in a fog. It's too dangerous.

Anderson weighs all of these factors and talks with Gray and Lambert. Last night's fog has lifted, but the wind is picking up. The water could be too choppy near the bridge-tunnel. And anyway, his scouting mission has revealed that gannets haven't arrived in great numbers. The crew makes a plan to stick to the shore and look for loons. They will have to wait for another night to catch gannets.

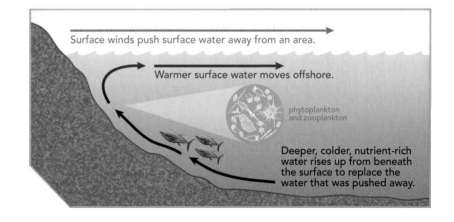

Surface winds push surface water away from an area.

Warmer surface water moves offshore.

phytoplankton and zooplankton

Deeper, colder, nutrient-rich water rises up from beneath the surface to replace the water that was pushed away.

CHAPTER 4
CHASING SEABIRDS

That evening the sky over the bay glows pink as the crew members take their usual places on board— Lambert on the prow, Gray behind him with the net, and Anderson at the wheel. The night is clear and calm—great weather for catching birds. The boat engines roar to life.

As the boat purrs through the bay, the air feels fresh and cold. Huge lighted ships are anchored in the middle of the bay. To the south, the lights of the bridge-tunnel sparkle.

Within minutes, Lambert spots a red-throated loon. The loon sees the boat and dives. The crew gives chase. The boat skims across the water. It kicks a shower of spray into the air. Anderson slows the boat and dims the lights as they approach the spot where the bird dived. Lambert sweeps the beam of light back and forth across the water, but the loon is nowhere to be seen.

"Spinning!" Anderson calls out a warning. The other two brace themselves as Anderson spins the boat in a tight circle. Lambert's beam of light traces a circular path over the water. Everyone looks, but no loon. Anderson kills the engines. The boat bobs in its own wake.

Scientists use different types of nets to catch seabirds for research. A large net is placed on the water with decoys to attract white-winged scoters (above), another type of sea duck off the Atlantic coast. To catch northern gannets and red-throated loons, the crew used a scoop net.

"It's the calm," says Anderson. "They can see us coming a mile way."

The crew continues on. They spot two gannets flying low over the water. The boat speeds after them, but the gannets fly on, too fast for the boat.

Then Lambert spots another loon in the beam of light. The boat approaches, and the loon dives. The boat spins. No loon. This loon, like the first one, has disappeared.

It happens in just a few seconds. Gray reaches over the side, dips the net into the water, and scoops up the resting bird. The gannet is in the net.

She hauls the seabird aboard. The bird lets out a deep *graaak*. Gray sits on a bench and holds the gannet in her lap. Lambert bands the bird. He gently wraps a lightweight metal band around its leg and squeezes the ends together with pliers. The band is stamped with a number. The band allows observers to see that this bird has been captured before and to find information about the species and the date and location of its capture.

Next, Gray and Lambert weigh the bird. Lambert wraps the bird's head in a towel to protect themselves from the saber-like beak. Together they slip the towel-wrapped bird into a nylon mesh bag and weigh it. They call out the number. Then they subtract the weight of the bag and the towel. Gray doesn't know if the bird is male or female. They look similar from the outside. But from the bird's weight, she guesses male. Male gannets are lighter than females. Anderson writes everything down: weight, band number, time, and capture location.

Carl Anderson keeps a firm hold on a gannet's beak. Gannets defend themselves with their sharp beaks and can injure crew members.

The sun is setting now. The boat *thrums*, sending ripples through the glassy surface. Lambert spots a gleaming white gannet awake on the water. The bird watches calmly as the boat glides up beside it.

THREATS TO SEABIRDS

No matter what effect offshore wind farms may have for birds, the ocean itself is changing in ways that harm seabirds, and people bear much of the responsibility. Seabirds get tangled in nets designed to snare fish. They swallow bits of plastic trash that float in the ocean. They aren't able to find enough food when large fishing boats take too many fish from the sea.

Climate change could bring even more significant changes to the ocean. As the climate warms, ocean water is growing warmer near the surface. In addition, the excess carbon dioxide in the air dissolves in seawater and forms an acid. This change is called ocean acidification.

Warmer, more acidic water can throw ocean food webs off-balance. Phytoplankton—the foundation of the ocean food web—thrive on cold, nutrient-rich waters that well up from the deep ocean. Warm surface water slows down these deep water upwellings. This leads to less food in the ocean. Acidification harms animals with shells, such as snails, clams, and

mussels. In more acidic seawater, these animals can't make their shells properly, so their shells are weaker. Weaker shells can mean the animal is more likely to get crushed or eaten. This can shift the relative amounts of different types of food. Some foods disappear, while others grow more abundant. All of these changes cascade through the food web.

These changes are clearly harming seabirds. What happens next will depend on actions people take now and in the future to prevent additional dangers.

Finally, Gray and Lambert slip the gannet into a large plastic tub. The tub has a raised platform inside made of mesh netting to keep the bird clean and dry. They are about to slide the lid in place when the bird pokes out its head and neck, stabbing with its beak. They gently wrestle the bird back into the tub and snap the lid in place.

Now begins a race against the clock. Too much time in captivity stresses the bird. The crew has just an hour to capture more birds before they must bring the seabird to shore.

Gray and Lambert switch jobs. Gray takes the spotlight, and Lambert holds the net. Anderson decides to head for the bridge-tunnel. If they caught one gannet, he says, maybe they'll have luck getting more.

Gradually the sparkling lights of the bridge-tunnel grow larger as the boat motors through the water. On the way, the crew spots more red-throated loons. They give chase. All escape.

Then they spot another red-throated loon. This one dives, swims, and comes up maybe 10 yards (9 m) from the boat. It spies the boat again. This time, it skids across the water—flapping, paddling, and trying to get away. Anderson pulls the boat up expertly beside it, and Lambert scoops the seabird into the net.

Gray and Lambert bend over the bird, working carefully with cold fingers to untangle its feathers from the net. The loon has a gray head, dark eyes, and charcoal feathers speckled white. Based on its appearance, Gray thinks it is a one-year-old bird. The bird remains calm as Lambert holds it in his lap and Gray weighs and bands it. She removes a feather that will be used to test later for mercury, a common poison in loons. Gray pricks one leg with a tiny needle to draw blood. The blood will be used to test whether the bird is male or female.

When she is finished, Gray gently drops the bird over the side of the boat. The loon gives a backward glance and swims away. The crew won't put a transmitter on a loon this young. Once a red-throated loon reaches adulthood, it has a good chance of surviving. But in the first three years of life, only about half of red-throated loons live through each year. The crew won't risk a tag on a bird that may not survive. Iain Stenhouse, one of the leaders on the project, later explained it this way: "The information that every tag brings in is so valuable, we don't want to risk losing that. We go to great lengths to try and make sure the [tagged] birds survive."

Meanwhile, back on the boat, the clock is ticking. The crew continues on toward the bridge-tunnel. It turns out to be a good move. They catch two more gannets. The last one puts up a good fight. It snaps its beak and lets out a deep *graaack*. Both Gray and Lambert have to help wrestle it into the tub.

Time is up. The crew has three gannets, an exciting catch for the night. They call the surgery team to let them know they are on their way. It is time to bring the seabirds to shore.

The team works quickly to weigh, tag, and draw blood from a captured loon *(above)*. A lightweight metal band is placed around the loon's leg (as Carrie Gray prepares to do, *below*). The band will identify the bird if it is ever caught again. Each bird is handled gently but quickly to minimize stress to the animal.

CHAPTER 5
RIDING THE WIND

The boat crew carries the jiggling plastic tubs into the rental house. One of the kitchens has been turned into an operating room. The surgery team—veterinarians Scott Ford, Michelle Kneeland, and Ginger Stout—bustles about getting ready. Ford, an experienced avian surgeon, will perform the surgery. Kneeland and Stout, both recent veterinary school graduates, will assist him.

Stout removes the first gannet from its box. *Graaak-graaak-graaak,* it croaks. Kneeland and Stout hold the male seabird while Ford examines it. He declares it to be perfectly healthy and gives it a sedative, putting the bird to sleep so he can implant a tracking device.

As they begin the surgery, Kneeland and Stout take turns monitoring the seabird's breathing and heart rate. Ford makes an incision and implants the tag into the bird's abdomen. The tag looks like two AA batteries side by side in a white mesh bag. An antenna sticks out of the bag.

As Ford works, he takes great care not to puncture the air sacs under the gannet's skin. These are vital for cushioning the impact when the seabird high-dives into the water. He makes a tiny hole near the tail for the antenna to poke out of the body. Then he sews up the seabird.

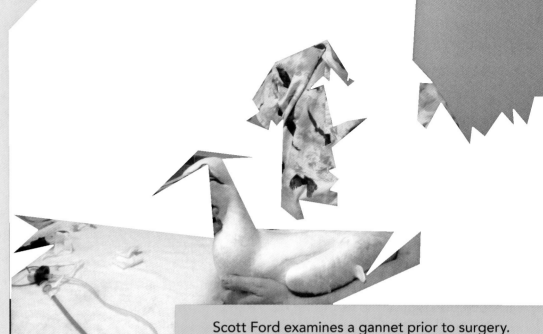
Scott Ford examines a gannet prior to surgery.

This tag is one type of transmitter implanted in surf scoters.

The birds recover after surgery and are released onto the water the next morning *(above)*. A released gannet may rest on the water before taking off *(below)*. Then the surgically implanted transmitter will reveal its travel patterns once in flight.

The implanted tag will send data to satellites orbiting Earth. The satellites will then send the information to computers to tell scientists where this bird travels.

As the surgery team implants tags in the other two gannets, the male gannet recovers in its box. The scientists will watch his movements for about one year until the tag batteries run down. They will learn his migration pathways and where he forages. The scientists will compare the movements of this gannet with the movements of other tagged gannets and look for patterns.

Before dawn, the scientists release all three seabirds on a quiet beach in Cape Charles. The male gannet flaps and runs across the water to get away. At a safe distance, he rests on the water and preens his feathers. Soon he will take flight.

In a few weeks, all the winter seabirds will leave these waters. The gannets will fly north to six colonies in eastern Canada. The red-throated loons will wing their way to the Arctic tundra. And the surf scoters will lift off in flocks to their breeding grounds across Canada and Alaska.

What will the tagged seabirds reveal? Where will they travel? Over the next year, the seabirds' tags will tell their stories.

FEATHER CARE 101

To survive in the ocean, seabirds need feathers in good working order. Feathers keep seabirds warm and dry, but caring for them takes daily effort. Seabirds fluff their feathers and comb them with their beaks. They smear on a waxy substance produced in a special gland to keep the feathers in good condition.

Feathers are key to survival after the surgery to implant a tag. When handling gannets, Scott Ford is careful to avoid damaging the feathers. Although he must smear a lubricant on the incision site, he always cleans the feathers thoroughly afterward.

Ford knows that caring for feathers takes a seabird's time and energy. In the ocean environment, how a seabird spends its energy is critical. A bird that spends too much energy cleaning its feathers could lose weight from not eating. It could fall victim to a predator. Survival, Ford says, is "all about energy balance."

Northern gannet colony

QUEBEC

Anticosti Island

Gulf of Saint Lawrence

Bonaventure Island

Bird Rocks

NEW BRUNSWICK

PRINCE EDWARD ISLAND

Cape Breton Island

Maine

NOVA SCOTIA

NEWFOUNDLAND

Funk Island

Baccalieu Island

Cape Saint Mary's

ATLANTIC OCEAN

CANADA

QUEBEC

Maine

NOVA SCOTIA

NEW BRUNSWICK

NEWFOUNDLAND

UNITED STATES

ATLANTIC OCEAN

NORTHERN GANNET BREEDING COLONIES

Gannets breed in six colonies in North America. Three are in the Gulf of Saint Lawrence, Quebec, and three are off the coast of Newfoundland.

waters at the outer edge of the continental shelf, where there is often an upwelling of cool, nutrient-rich, and food-filled water. After a few days, he circles back to the Chesapeake.

On April 2, he begins his migration. He glides on winds blowing north and follows the continental shelf edge. When he spots a school of fish, he rockets downward and spears the water with a splash. He may gulp his catch underwater, or he may bring his prey to the surface, shake it, toss it, juggle it, and swallow. If he catches no fish, he returns immediately to the air and prepares for another dive.

After a week and a half, the seabird arrives at Cape Saint Mary's in Canada, on the shores of Newfoundland. His tag reveals that he has flown a distance of more than 1,250 miles (2,015 km) in ten days.

The tagging data reveals only the male gannet's location, not what he is doing. But Iain Stenhouse has spent years observing

For the last few weeks of March, the tagged male gannet stays near the mouth of the Chesapeake. Like other gannets, he probably spends most of his time gliding over the waves and looking for fish under the rippling water. On one occasion, the male seabird visits the bountiful fishing

seabirds at their colonies, and he has a pretty good idea of what life is like at the colony.

"It's a complete commotion all the time," says Stenhouse. "These birds are all milling around in the air, with birds landing and birds taking off. And everybody seems to be squawkin'. At sea you rarely hear a gannet make a sound, but in the colony they're very vocal."

At the Cape Saint Mary's colony, as with other seabird colonies, an overpowering smell hangs in the air. It is the fishy smell of guano, seabird poop. The nests are spaced evenly on the rocky ground, like honeycomb in a beehive. Each gannet defends its nest site with jabs at its neighbors. By nesting close together, the gannets protect themselves and their chicks from predators. In such close company, however, they quarrel often and fights break out.

Life at the Cape Saint Mary's colony is a noisy commotion. Gannets nest close together on the rocky ground and fish in the nearby waters.

THE SLOW LIVES OF SEABIRDS

Seabirds live long, slow lives. Northern gannets can live for twenty years or more. However, they don't begin breeding until the age of five, and they raise just one chick a year, which requires the constant efforts of both parents. Surviving the early years of life is tricky, and many young gannets never reach adulthood.

Their long lives and slow reproduction make seabirds vulnerable to wind farms. A small decline in adult survival could cause the entire population to fall.

WILDLIFE SURVEYS

Not only seabirds could be vulnerable to offshore wind farms. Sea turtles, whales, and dolphins could also be affected, although scientists don't know what species are likely to come into contact with Atlantic wind farms. To learn more, the research team surveyed, or counted, wildlife off the coasts of Delaware, Maryland, and Virginia. Their 5,113 square-mile (13,245 sq. km) survey area was chosen because it contains three Wind Energy Areas. Some scientists counted wildlife from a boat as it zigzagged across the survey area. Others counted wildlife from video footage, shot from a plane with four powerful video cameras mounted on the bottom. They combined the boat and aerial survey data to get a complete picture of all the wildlife in the area.

Scientists observed a wide variety of animals, such as right whales (below), one of the most endangered large whales in the world. These enormous animals migrate along the US and Canadian Atlantic coast. Right whales use sound to communicate and are at risk from noise during wind farm construction. Conservation groups and wind farm developers are working together to protect right whales.

Project leader Kate Williams says the surveys and bird tagging data complement each other. The surveys give a snapshot of where animals

are located at one time. Tagging gives detailed information about how individual seabirds are moving. By combining the two, "We can actually start getting a really good feel for where animals are hanging out, how they're moving," says Williams. "We can start looking for patterns."

"They nest together by the thousands . . . because they *have* to and not because they *want* to," says Stenhouse. "They don't like each other, the way they behave. They'll just as easily take their neighbor's eye out as ignore them."

The male gannet and his mate meet at their nest site. Gannets mate for life and return to the same nest site year after year. The female lays a single egg in May or June. In the noisy colony, the two take turns caring for the egg. One parent keeps the egg warm under its webbed feet while the other travels far across the waves and fills up on summer's bounty of fish. After six weeks, the tiny chick hatches. It grows quickly on a diet of regurgitated fish brought by its parents. At three months old, the chick is ready to hunt on its own. It splashes along with the other chicks into the sea. At first, it cannot fly and must begin its migration by swimming. Within a week or two, its wings grow stronger, and it continues its journey from the air.

By early October, a chilly fall wind is blowing across the colony. From the male's tag, scientists can see that he forages widely, traveling far over the waves but always returning to the colony. Finally, he senses it is time to return to his winter home. On October 24, he catches the wind and flies south along the continental shelf. He powers his flight with wind under his wings, watches for fish with his sharp eyes, and splashes into the water in daring dives. He pauses for two months near the coast of Maine and Massachusetts, flying back and forth between the shelf edge and the shoreline. In January he continues on, winging his way south. Past Connecticut and New York he flies, past New Jersey, past Delaware. In February he arrives back at his winter home, the rich fishing waters of the Chesapeake Bay.

A male and female gannet nestle each other and their chick. The downy chick cannot yet fly and depends on its parents to bring it a diet of fish.

CHAPTER 6
BETWEEN SKY AND SEA

For four years, scientists chased, caught, and tagged Atlantic seabirds. They watched the flight path of each tagged individual. Then they looked at that bird's movements together with the paths of other tagged members of its species. They compared those movements with changes in the seasons and weather, and looked for patterns. The tagging data is being collected in databases.

A male surf scoter feeds on a mussel. In winter, surf scoters feed in shallow waters where they dive for shellfish.

The scientists' hard work has created a much clearer picture of how seabirds use the middle Atlantic Ocean. The researchers learned that red-throated loons hunt for fish in bays and in shallow waters near the shore. They migrate by flying along the coast. Surf scoters dive for mollusks in bays and along the shore, and they also migrate along the coast.

Northern gannets carry out their spectacular dives along the shore, mostly in or near large bays. Although they often venture near shore, they don't stay there. They journey widely over the continental shelf. During migration, some gannets fly along the coast. Other gannets follow the edge of the continental shelf, which brings them as close as 18 miles (29 km) offshore in North Carolina and as far as 124 miles (200 km) offshore in northern New England.

Through this research, scientists gained important insight into the lives of seabirds. And they obtained vital data for guiding safe wind farm development. The tag data shows that some parts of the mid-Atlantic region—like nearshore waters and the mouths of bays—are very important to seabirds. Seabirds may be most at risk if wind farms are placed close to these areas.

Government officials and industry leaders can use these new insights to minimize harm

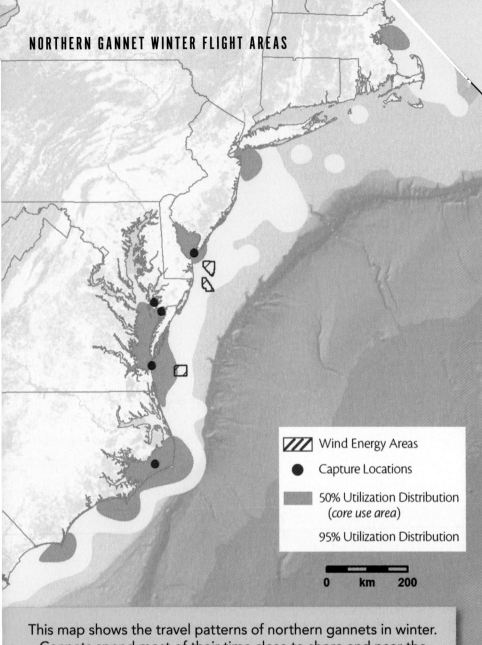

Wind Energy Areas

● Capture Locations

50% Utilization Distribution (core use area)

95% Utilization Distribution

0   km   200

This map shows the travel patterns of northern gannets in winter. Gannets spend most of their time close to shore and near the mouths of bays (areas shown in orange). But they also roam over wide areas of the continental shelf (shown in yellow). Dots show where scientists captured gannets to tag, and the dark outlines show the areas being considered for wind farm development.

to birds from offshore wind farms. The knowledge scientists have gained will help keep seabirds safe as offshore wind farms begin to bring clean energy to coastal areas.

Still, experts worry because gannets roam so widely. The birds' travels could bring them into contact with wind farms anywhere along the continental shelf. This raises a complicated question. If a gannet flew near a wind farm, would it be at risk of collision? Or might it avoid the area altogether? If gannets avoid wind farms, that could decrease winter habitat for them, making them have to compete harder for food in other areas. Or wind farms could present an obstacle on their migration. If gannets have to spend extra energy taking the long way around wind farms, they could arrive at their nesting grounds thinner and with less energy for reproducing. Lower energy might lead to fewer eggs laid or a drop in the survival rate of chicks, which could lead to a decline in population.

Clearly, experts' concerns about seabirds and wind farms include a lot of ifs. No one yet knows how wind farms will affect gannets. Scientists will continue to ask more questions and do more research.

In the twenty-first century, seabirds face many threats. Plastic trash, fishing nets, and overfishing all pose serious dangers. Climate change threatens to radically alter marine habitats. Most changes in climate or habitat are slow and gradual, over thousands or tens of thousands of years, giving birds time to adapt. But the changes that people are making to the oceans are happening in a heartbeat, by comparison, and seabirds may not have time to adapt.

To protect seabirds, people need to be good stewards of the ocean. Offshore wind could even help seabirds, by providing a source of energy that doesn't pollute, but it must be done in a bird-safe way. If everyone works together—from scientists who study seabirds to people who read books about them—we can harness offshore wind power while keeping the ocean safe, and these birds will still be out there, flying between the sky and the sea.

SEABIRDS AND THE SCIENTIFIC PROCESS

The research team used the scientific method to help them learn more about seabirds. Their first step was to ask a question: What birds could be at risk from wind farms in the mid-Atlantic Ocean? Their next step was to do background research. They looked at what parts of the ocean were being targeted for wind farms. They studied which birds lived nearby. They researched how similar birds had responded to offshore wind farms in Europe.

Then the scientists developed hypotheses, or predictions of what they would find. They chose three species of seabirds that could be at risk. They designed an experiment to capture and tag the seabirds and carried it out.

Later, they analyzed their data. They looked for patterns to help them understand the movements of each species. Based on their data, they made predictions about where each species was likely to be and how likely each was to come into contact with future wind farms. Their research also created more questions.

Finally, they communicated their results, sharing their findings with other scientists, government officials, and the public.

SAVING THE OCEAN

Protecting the ocean is a big job, too big for scientists and politicians alone. It takes many people working together to make a difference. You can take action in your own home and community to help.

Be aware of your energy use at home and school. Saving energy is one of the most important steps you can take to protect the oceans. Much of the world's energy still comes from fossil fuels—oil, coal, and natural gas. Saving energy cuts down on the carbon dioxide pollution that is contributing to global warming and harming the oceans.

Use less plastic. Plastic trash often ends up being blown or washed out to sea, where it threatens seabirds and other marine animals. Carry a reusable water bottle, bring cloth bags when you shop, and don't buy products with a lot of plastic packaging.

If you eat fish, choose seafood that has been sustainably harvested. Many species are being pushed to extinction by overfishing. Not only is this bad for fish, it harms ocean food webs. Learn what fish is still abundant and caught by methods that don't harm marine wildlife. You can learn more at http://www.seafoodwatch.org.

Support groups that are working to protect ocean habitat and marine wildlife. Learn about ocean creatures, what threatens them, and how you can protect them. Then share your knowledge so you can educate and inspire others.

AUTHOR'S NOTE AND ACKNOWLEDGMENTS

I have spent many summer days on mid-Atlantic beaches—riding waves, building sand sculptures, eating saltwater taffy. I love to wake early and watch the sun rise over the water, while dolphins swim by or birds fly out to the horizon and disappear from sight.

The fact that seabirds live over the ocean and come to land only once a year amazes me. So does the fact that these birds—hidden from human eyes—are completely unknown to most people. Yet people need to know about them. Seabirds have been on Earth much longer than people have, and their lives depend on how well we take care of their ocean home.

I was thrilled to have the chance to tell this story of modern science research. But this book would not have been possible without the help of many people.

First, I would like to thank Iain Stenhouse, who first told me about the mid-Atlantic seabird study during an interview. He has been a strong supporter of this book along the way and has answered endless questions about seabirds, seabird colonies, bird tagging, and the ocean environment.

Both he and Kate Williams gave assistance with the manuscript, for which I am grateful. Any errors or inaccuracies that remain are gaps in my knowledge, not theirs.

I am deeply indebted to all the scientists, field-workers, and veterinarians, as well as others involved with this study, who discussed the project with me; welcomed me into their work, onto their boat, and into their operating room; and who shared their insights, knowledge, and data with me. Many are mentioned in the book. A few others that I would like to thank are Emily Connelly, Deb McKew, and Sarah Johnson of the Biodiversity Research Institute; and Caleb Spiegel of the US Fish and Wildlife Service.

In addition, I am grateful to my editors, Carol Hinz and Anna Cavallo, for their wise guidance from draft to book.

Finally, I would like to thank my husband, Rick, and our daughters, Anna, Eva, and Ellie, who have cheered on this project, asked thoughtful questions about seabirds, and listened to my answers. I appreciate their ongoing support.

SOURCE NOTES

5   Iain Stenhouse, interview with the author, September 29, 2015.

7   Iain Stenhouse, e-mail interview with author, November 23, 2015.

9   Carrie Gray, interview with the author, March 11, 2015.

9   Carl Anderson, interview with the author, March 11, 2015.

13 Carl Anderson, interview with the author, September 29, 2014.

16 Ibid.

16 Ibid.

17 Anderson, interview, March 11, 2015.

17 Gray, interview.

17 Robby Lambert, interview with the author, March 11, 2015.

17 Gray, interivew.

17 Anderson, interview, March 11, 2015.

25 Ibid.

25 Ibid.

28 Ibid.

28 Ibid.

29 Iain Stenhouse, interview with the author, September 11, 2015.

33 Scott Ford, interview with the author, March 12, 2015.

35 Iain Stenhouse, interview with the author, January 27, 2014.

36 Ibid.

36 Kate Williams, interview with the author, November 21, 2013.

GLOSSARY

carbon dioxide: an invisible gas that is exhaled by humans and many other living things and that is released when fossil fuels are burned

continental shelf: the flat, shallow edge of a continent that is submerged under the sea and extends to an edge that slopes downward to the ocean floor

current: a stream of water that flows continuously in one direction

ecosystem: a community of different living things interacting with their natural environment

fossil fuel: a fuel, such as coal, oil, or natural gas, that was formed in the past from the remains of plants or animals

global positioning system (GPS): a device that uses satellite signals to find the exact location of something on Earth

global warming: a warming of Earth's atmosphere and oceans caused by an increase in greenhouse gases such as carbon dioxide

habitat: the place where a plant or animal normally lives or grows

mollusk: a group of animals, such as snails and clams, with a soft body usually enclosed in a hard shell

northern gannet: a large seabird that breeds in colonies on both sides of the Atlantic and is known for its high-speed dives

nutrient: a substance that provides nourishment essential for life

ocean acidification: the process by which ocean water comes to contain more acid, caused by the uptake of carbon dioxide from the air

phytoplankton: tiny marine plants that drift in ocean water and are food for a wide range of ocean animals including zooplankton, fish, and whales

population: a group of a species of organisms living in a particular area or habitat

predator: an animal that lives by killing and eating other animals

preen: to groom feathers with the beak

red-throated loon: a medium-sized seabird that breeds in the Arctic and winters in northern coastal waters around the world

species: a unique type of living organism

surf scoter: a large sea duck that breeds in Alaska and Canada and winters on coasts in the northern United States

survey: to find out the number, identity, and position of the wildlife in a particular area

tundra: a cold, treeless plain having a permanently frozen layer below the ground

upwelling: the process of deeper, cooler, nutrient-rich ocean water moving to the ocean surface

wind farm: an area of land or water with a group of energy-producing wind turbines

wind turbine: an engine with blades that are rotated by the wind to produce electricity

zooplankton: tiny marine mammals that drift or swim in ocean water and feed on other zooplankton or phytoplankton

SELECTED BIBLIOGRAPHY

American Wind Energy Association. Accessed April 8, 2016. http://www.awea.org.

Berlin, Jeremy. "Daring Divers." *National Geographic,* August 2012, 68–75.

The Birds of North America Online. Cornell Lab of Ornithology. Accessed September 30, 2015. http://bna.birds.cornell.edu/bna/.

Lippson, Alice Jane, and Robert L. Lippson. *Life in the Chesapeake Bay.* Baltimore: Johns Hopkins University Press, 2006.

"Offshore Wind Energy." Bureau of Ocean Energy Management. Accessed December 1, 2013. http://www.boem.gov/Renewable
    -Energy-Program/Renewable-Energy-Guide/Offshore-Wind-Energy.aspx.

"Offshore Wind Power." National Wildlife Foundation. Accessed September 10, 2015. https://www.nwf.org/What-We-Do/Energy
    -and-Climate/Renewable-Energy/Offshore-Wind.aspx.

Safina, Carl. "How Climate Change Is Sinking Seabirds." *Audubon,* September/October 2014. Accessed April 13, 2016. https://
    www.audubon.org/magazine/september-october-2014/how-climate-change-sinking-seabirds.

Sibley, David Allen. *The Sibley Guide to Bird Life & Behavior.* New York: Alfred A. Knopf, 2001.

Weidensaul, Scott. *Living on the Wind: Across the Hemisphere with Migratory Birds.* New York: North Point, 1999.

White, Christopher P. *Chesapeake Bay Nature of the Estuary: A Field Guide.* Centreville, MD: Tidewater, 1989.

Williams, Kate A., Emily E. Connelly, Sarah M. Johnson, and Iain J. Stenhouse. "Wildlife Densities and Habitat Use across
    Temporal and Spatial Scales on the Mid-Atlantic Outer Continental Shelf." Biodiversity Research Institute. October 2015.
    http://www.briloon.org/mabs/reports.

Williams, Kate A., Iain J. Stenhouse, Emily E. Connelly, and Sarah M. Johnson. "Mid-Atlantic Wildlife Studies: Distribution and
    Abundance of Wildlife along the Eastern Seaboard 2012–2014." Biodiversity Research Institute. Accessed October 10, 2015.
    http://www.briloon.org/mabs/reports.

FURTHER INFORMATION

Biodiversity Research Institute
    http://www.briloon.org
    This is the official site for the Biodiversity Research Institute, the group of scientists that is coordinating the study of
    mid-Atlantic seabirds.

Cornell Lab of Ornithology—All about Birds
    http://www.birds.cornell.edu/
    Want to hear what the birds in this book sound like? Go to this site and type the name of a bird into the search box. You'll also
    discover many cool facts about each species.

Department of Energy—How a Wind Turbine Works
    http://energy.gov/articles/how-wind-turbine-works
    Go to this site to learn how a wind turbine works.

Energy Kids—Wind
    http://www.eia.gov/kids/energy.cfm?page=wind_home-basics
    Learn more about wind energy and how a wind turbine works on this site from the US Energy Information Administration.

Environmental Protection Agency—Frequently Asked Questions about Climate Change
    http://www3.epa.gov/climatechange/kids/faq.html
    Confused about climate change? This site has a list of frequently asked questions that can help set you straight.

Hoose, Phillip. *Moonbird: A Year on the Wind with the Great Survivor B95.* New York: Farrar, Straus and Giroux, 2012. This book is all about the migration and conservation of a celebrated bird of the Atlantic shore, the rufa red knot.

National Geographic—"Daring Divers"
    http://ngm.nationalgeographic.com/2012/08/gannets/berlin-text
    See stunning photos of the northern gannet, and watch a video of the closely related cape gannet diving for fish.

National Geographic—"The Ocean"
    http://ocean.nationalgeographic.com/ocean/
    Learn more about what lives in the ocean and how to protect it.

Newman, Patricia. *Plastic, Ahoy! Investigating the Great Pacific Garbage Patch.* Minneapolis: Millbrook Press, 2014. A research team investigates plastic pollution in the ocean and how it is impacting ocean wildlife.

NOAA—"Seabirds"
    http://www.gc.noaa.gov/gcil_seabirds.html
    Learn more about the wide world of seabirds and the threats they face on this site from the National Oceanic and Atmospheric Administration.

Smithsonian—"Gannets Plunge into the Sea"
    http://www.smithsonianmag.com/videos/category/science/gannets-plunge-into-the-sea/?no-ist
    Watch spectacular video footage above and below the water showing a flock of cape gannets high-speed diving for sardines.

Smithsonian—"How You Can Help the Ocean"
    http://ocean.si.edu/ocean-news/how-you-can-help-ocean
    Read this thoughtful list of suggestions for what you can do from the Smithsonian National Museum of Natural History.

Turner, Pamela S. *Prowling the Seas: Exploring the Hidden World of Ocean Predators.* New York: Walker, 2009. This book highlights the effort to tag four Pacific Ocean predators—sharks, tuna, sea turtles, and a pair of seabirds—to learn more about their habits and long-distance movements.

Webb, Sophie. *Far from Shore: Chronicles of an Open Sea Voyage.* New York: Houghton Mifflin, 2011. Join a scientific voyage and learn about a wide range of ocean wildlife, including seabirds, dolphins, fish, and whales.

INDEX

PHOTO ACKNOWLEDGMENTS

The images in this book are used with the permission of: © iStockphoto.com/pchoui (Silhouetted bird head); © iStockphoto.com/Patrick Ellis (Silhouetted wind turbine); © Tom Vezo/Minden Pictures, p. 1; © Markus Varesvuo/Minden Pictures, p. 4; © Richard Shucksmith/Minden Pictures, p. 5; © Wolfgang Kaehler/LightRocket/Getty Images, p. 6 (top); © All Canada Photos/Alamy, p. 6 (bottom); © Ann & Steve Toon/Robert Harding World Imagery/Corbis, p. 7 (top); © iStockphoto.com/Steve Bridge, p. 7 (bottom); © iStockphoto.com/Bob Balestri, p. 8; BRI-Jonathan Fiely, pp. 10, 19, 29 (top), 30; © Laura Westlund/Independent Picture Service, pp. 11, 12, 23, 34; © iStockphoto.com/ Tomasz Wyszołmirski, p. 12 (background); © iStockphoto.com/GregC, p. 13; © Ken Archer/DanitaDelimont.com/Getty Images, p. 14; © iStockphoto.com/pchoui, p. 15 (top); © Paul Hobson/Minden Pictures, p. 15 (middle); © All Canada Photos/Alamy, p. 15 (bottom); © Jasper Doest/Minden Pictures, p. 16; © L. Toshio Kishiyama/Flickr RF/Getty Images, p. 18; © Carl Purcell/Alamy, p. 20; © RosaBetancourt 0 people images/Alamy, p. 21 (bottom); © FLPA/Alamy, p. 21 (top); © BRI, pp. 22, 40; © iStockphoto.com/Yvonne Navalaney, p. 24; BRI-Peter Paton, p. 25; BRI-Carl Anderson, pp. 26, 29 (top), 31, 32 (all), 41; © Buiten-Beeld/Alamy, p. 27; © Jasper Doest/Minden Pictures, p. 33; © John Barger/Alamy, p. 35; © David L. Ryan/The Boston Globe/Getty Images, p. 36; © Yva Momatiuk and John Eastcott/Minden Pictures, p. 37; © Marie Read/Minden Pictures, p. 38; © Jan Wegener/Minden Pictures, p. 39; © Bill Coster/Minden Pictures, p. 42 (left); © iStockphoto.com/Jennifer Byron, p. 42 (right).

Front cover: © iStockphoto.com/Kneonlight (bird in flight); © iStockphoto.com/HoleInTheBucket (wind turbines).

Back cover: © iStockphoto.com/Thomas-Mertens.